CW00542997

GOURMET RECIPES FOR BEGINNERS

DINNER

Gustav Mancini

Welcome!

..to this new series of book, inspired by all the recipes I know thanks to my great passion, **cooking!**

In this book you will find many different ideas for your dishes, with ingredients from all around the world, with a Gourmet touch!

Thanks to these cookbooks you can develop your cooking skills for any kind of meal,

as you'll find recipes for:

- Lunch
- Dinner
- Salads
- Desserts
- And much more...

Whether your favourite dish is French fries, muffins, chicken tenders or grilled vegetables, with this series of books you will learn how to do it with a better-looking touch!

If you think that it will be difficult to prepare a dish in a gourmet way, you will discover that it doesn't need that much to change the look of it.

Don't forget that this books have also low fat recipes with healthy ingredients to *keep you fit and have a healthier meal plan!*

Remember that having a wide variety of ingredients and foods in your diet have many benefits for you, that's why you will find ingredients from:

- Asia
- Russia
- America
- Europe
- And more...

Since I started to pay more attention on the decision of the ingredients and how to plate a dish, I enjoy cooking a lot more! That's why I made this cookbook for all of you that want to develop your cooking skills and start eating healthier!

I hope you will enjoy this book and don't forget to check out the other ones from the collection, and enjoy your time in the kitchen!

GOURMET RECIPES FOR BEGINNERS: SIDES

Learn how to cook delicious sides to enjoy your meals! This cookbook contains classy recipes to cook step-by-step, ideal to build a healthy and delicious meal plan, but also perfect for your events and parties!

GOURMET RECIPES FOR BEGINNERS: DESSERTS

Learn how to cook quick desserts to give your day a good flavour! This cookbook contains easy but selected recipes to prepare step-by-step delicious desserts, snacks and pies, with fruit and other ingredients, Perfect for your events, parties and aperitifs or simply at the end of your dinner!

GOURMET RECIPES FOR BEGINNERS: SALADS

Learn how to cook yummy salads for a complete meal plan! This cookbook contains easy but selected recipes to prepare step-by-step, perfect for your daily meals, parties or aperitifs either. Lose weight by eating well with the right recipe book, for a healthy diet and body-healing.

GOURMET RECIPES FOR BEGINNERS: BREAD

Learn how to cook yummy bread recipes to enjoy daily meals! This cookbook contains easy but classy recipes to prepare step-by-step, perfect for your home cooking or aperitifs either.
Bread backing becomes easy with the right recipe book!

GOURMET RECIPES FOR BEGINNERS: LUNCH

Learn how to cook yummy recipes to enjoy your main meals! This cookbook contains easy but selected dishes to prepare step-by-step, perfect for your home, parties or aperitifs either. Lose weight by eating well with the right recipe book, for a healthy and complete diet!

GOURMET RECIPES FOR BEGINNERS: DINNER

Learn how to cook yummy recipes to enjoy your main meals! This cookbook contains easy but classy dishes to prepare step-by-step, perfect for your home cooking, parties or aperitifs either. Lose weight by eating well with the right recipe book, for a healthy and healing diet!

GOURMET RECIPES FOR BEGINNERS:QUICK AND EASY

Learn how to cook delicious quick-and-easy recipes. This cookbook contains simple but classy dishes to prepare step-by-step, perfect for your home cooking, parties or aperitifs either. Lose weight by eating well with the right recipe book, for a healthy and TIME-SAVING diet!

GOURMET RECIPES FOR BEGINNERS: APPETIZERS

Learn how to cook tasty snacks to enjoy your free time! With many and different ingredients, this cookbook contains more than 50 appetizer recipes to cook step-by-step, ideal to build a healthy and delicious daily meal plan, but also perfect for your events, parties and aperitifs!!

FRESH AND HEALHTY SALADS AND APPETIZERS

2 BOOKS IN **1**: gourmet recipes for beginners salads and appetizers. This cookbook contains simple but classy meals to prepare step-by-step, perfect for your home cooking, parties or aperitifs either. Lose weight by eating well with the right recipe book, for a complete and TIME-SAVING diet!

COMPLETE MEAL PLAN FOR BEGINNERS

3 BOOKS IN **1**: gourmet recipes lunch, dinner and desserts. This cookbook contains quick and easy meals to prepare step-by-step, perfect for your home cooking, parties or aperitifs either. Lose weight by eating well with the right recipe book, for a complete and healthy diet!

GUSTAV MANCINI

gourmet recipes
for beginners

LEARN HOW TO COOK YUMMY RECIPES TO ENJOY YOUR MAIN MEALS! This cookbook contains easy but classy dishes to prepare step-by-step, perfect for your home cooking, parties or aperitifs either. Lose weight by eating well with the right recipe book, for a healthy and healing diet!

DINNER

Table of Contents

SURPRISE SOMEONE WITH A FANCY DINNER 16

Chinese Stir Fried Sticky Rice With Chinese Sausage.. 17

Cilantro Chutney Chicken 21

Citrus Pork Tenderloin 24

Coquilles St. Jacques 27

Cordon Bleu Rollups With Honey Mustard Wine Sauce
.... 30

Cornish Game Hens With Garlic And Rosemary 34

Cornish Hens The Easy Way 37

Crab Croissants 39

Crab Stuffed Lobster Tail..41

Cracked Black Venison 44

Creamy Chicken Marsala Fettuccine........................... 46

Creamy Saffron Shrimp With Gnocchi And Caramelized
Onion.. 50

Crispy Chinese Noodles With Eggplant And Peanuts . 53

Cuban Pork Roast II 57

Cuban Shredded Pork..59

Deviled Crab 62

Dill Poached Salmon 65

Dry Brined Smoked Salmon.....................................67

Duck Breasts With Raspberry Sauce 70

Duck Cassoulet 73

Easy Chicken Korma 76

Easy Prime Rib Roast...79

Eggless Pasta...82

Eggs Benedict With Salmon 84

Erin's Indonesian Chicken 87

Father In Law's Scallops With Sun Dried Tomatoes And
Bacon... 89

Fennel Risotto...92

Feta And Olive Meatballs 94

Fettuccine In Creamy Mushroom And Sage Sauce 96

Filipino Ribs 98

Fish Baked En Croute De Sel (Fish Baked In A Salt Crust)..101

Fish Roll Ups... 104

Foolproof Rib Roast..107

Fresh Figs And Di Parma Pizza 109

Fruit 'n' Honey Granola 112

Garlicky Vodka Alfredo.. 115

Genuine Egg Noodles 117

Ginger Glazed Mahi Mahi... 119

Gkai Kamin 122

Glazed Corned Beef...124

Goat Cheese Stuffed Chicken 126

Gorgonzola And Wild Mushroom Risotto 130

Gourmet Pub Burgers..133

....136

THANK YOU..137

SURPRISE SOMEONE WITH A FANCY DINNER

Chinese Stir Fried Sticky Rice With Chinese Sausage

Serving: 6

Ingredients

- 2 dried scallops
- 2 teaspoons dark soy sauce
- 1 teaspoon white sugar
- 1 teaspoon olive oil
- 3 eggs, beaten
- 3 links Chinese sausage, diced
- 2 cups glutinous rice
- 8 dried shiitake mushrooms
- 1/3 cup dried shrimp
- 2 cups hot water, or more as needed
- 2 tablespoons light soy sauce, or to taste

- 1/2 cup chopped cilantro, or to taste

Direction

- In a big bowl with water, submerge rice for approximately 4 hours till mostly clear. Wash and drain well.

- In 3 individual bowls with water, submerge scallops, shrimp and mushrooms for around 15 minutes till softened. Drain, setting aside mushroom liquid and throwing away the other water. Cut scallops, shrimp and mushrooms into small portions.

- In a big skillet, heat the olive oil on medium heat. Into the skillet, add eggs, swirling to spread out into a thin layer. Cook for around a minute till mostly set. Turn over and cook for 3 to 5 minutes till not runny anymore.

- Turn out the egg onto a cutting board and cool slightly. Roll into a long tube and cut into thin ribbons.

- Into the same skillet, mix Chinese sausage on medium heat. Cook and mix for around 3 minutes till aromatic and some of oil is rendered. Put in scallops, shrimp and mushrooms; let it cook for 3 minutes to 5 minutes. Turn out mixture of sausage onto a bowl.

- Into the skillet, mix the drained rice. Cook and mix for 1 to 2 minutes till slightly toasted. Add the reserved mushroom liquid, mixing continuously till water is absorbed. Put in hot water, half a cup at a time, mixing till water is absorbed among every addition. Cook for approximately 25 minutes till rice softens.

- Season the rice with sugar, dark soy sauce and light soy sauce. Mix in the sausage mixture and egg ribbons. Put cilantro on top prior to serving.

Nutrition Information

- Calories: 545 calories;

- Cholesterol: 104

- Protein: 21.8

- Total Fat: 16.4

- Sodium: 831

- Total Carbohydrate: 82.8

Cilantro Chutney Chicken

Serving: 4

Ingredients

- 1 bunch fresh cilantro

- 1 teaspoon ground cumin

- 1 jalapeno chile pepper, stem and seeds removed

- 1 (3 pound) whole chicken, cut into pieces

- 2 teaspoons minced fresh ginger root

- 2 teaspoons minced garlic

- 2 tablespoons lemon juice

- 1/4 cup ground unsalted cashews

- 1 cup heavy whipping cream

- salt to taste

Direction

- Start preheating the oven to 350°F (175°C).

- Discard and remove chicken skin. Rinse parts then pat dry. Combine ginger and garlic; then rub over chicken. Put chicken parts into a 9x13 in. baking dish, cover in foil. Put aside.

- In the meantime, in a blender, put lemon juice, jalapeno chile pepper, cumin and cilantro. Puree until they become smooth, if necessary, pouring in more water. Put aside for later. Combine cashews in a separate small bowl with cream. Stir well then add over the chicken.

- Bake chicken for half an hour at 350°F (175°C), or until the juices release. Then bake, uncovered about 15 mins longer, letting liquid in the dish slightly thicken to a gravy.

- Take out of the oven. Mix gravy in the dish with reserved cilantro chutney. Mix well. Add over chicken to serve.

Nutrition Information

- Calories: 997 calories;

- Sodium: 270

- Total Carbohydrate: 6.6

- Cholesterol: 337

- Protein: 66.4

- Total Fat: 77.5

Citrus Pork Tenderloin

Serving: 8

Ingredients

- salt and ground black pepper to taste

- 3 blood oranges, halved

- 1 cup fruity white wine, such as sauvignon blanc

- 2 pork tenderloins

- 2 cloves garlic, sliced, or more to taste

- 1/4 cup coarsely chopped cilantro

- 1 tablespoon cornstarch

- 1/2 cup cold water

Direction

- Set an oven to 200°C (400°F) and start preheating.

- Use a sharp paring knife to make a small shallow slit in the pork tenderloins, then stuff into each slit with a slice of garlic. Flavor the pork with black pepper and salt, then put into a 9x13-inch glass baking dish. Squeeze the blood orange halves onto the pork; keep 2-3 squeezed halves in the baking dish. Add the white wine onto the pork and scatter with cilantro.

- In the prepared oven, bake for half an hour until an instant-read meat thermometer registers 65°C (150°F) when inserted in the thickest part of a tenderloin. Let the pork rest for 5-10 minutes.

- Remove the baked orange rinds when resting the pork, then fill a small saucepan with pan juices. Boil the juices. In a small bowl, beat cornstarch and cold water together until smooth; add into the pan juices and stir. Turn down the heat to low, allow the sauce to simmer for 5 minutes until it thickens. To serve, slice the pork into thin medallions, then put the sauce on top.

Nutrition Information

- Calories: 186 calories;
- Protein: 21.2
- Total Fat: 4.3
- Sodium: 47
- Total Carbohydrate: 9.4
- Cholesterol: 63

Coquilles St. Jacques

Serving: 4

Ingredients

- 1 pound sea scallops, quartered
- 1/2 pound button mushrooms, sliced
- 1/2 cup chopped onion
- 1 cup mayonnaise
- 1/4 cup dry white wine
- 1 tablespoon chopped fresh parsley
- 1/2 cup dry bread crumbs
- 5 tablespoons melted butter
- 6 ounces shredded Gruyere cheese

Direction

- Toss the bread crumbs with 1 tablespoon of melted butter in a small mixing bowl; mix thoroughly; put aside.

- Mix parsley, wine, mayonnaise and cheese in another small bowl; mix thoroughly; put aside.

- Sauté scallops in 2 tablespoons of melted butter until opaque over medium heat in a skillet. Place onto a plate lined with paper towels. Set the broiler for medium/high heat and start preheating.

- Over medium heat, reheat the skillet; cook the onion and mushrooms in 2 tbsp. of melted butter until tender. Add cheese mixture; transfer the scallops bake to the skillet. Cook until cheese is melted and scallops are heated through. Scoop the mixture into separate ramekins or transfer the entire mixture into an 11x7 inch baking dish. Scatter over with bread crumbs mixture.

- Broil in the prepared broiler 6 inches from heat for 2-4 minutes or until browned.

Nutrition Information

- Calories: 888 calories;

- Protein: 35.6

- Total Fat: 73.7

- Sodium: 842

- Total Carbohydrate: 19.6

- Cholesterol: 143

Cordon Bleu Rollups With Honey Mustard Wine Sauce

Serving: 8

Ingredients

- 1/2 pound sliced Swiss cheese

- 3 tablespoons honey

- 1 tablespoon prepared horseradish

- salt and pepper to taste

- 2 cups white wine

- 1 teaspoon chopped fresh tarragon

- 1/2 pound sliced cooked ham

- 2 tablespoons brown sugar, divided

- salt and pepper to taste

- 1 tablespoon all-purpose flour

- 2 cups white wine

- 1/4 cup Dijon mustard

- 1 teaspoon chopped fresh parsley

- 1 tablespoon olive oil

- 1 pound skinless, boneless chicken breast halves

Direction

- To marinate: In a non-porous glass bowl or dish, combine oil, parsley, tarragon, and 2 cups of wine. Put in chicken and toss it to coat. Put a cover on the bowl or dish, then marinate in the fridge for at least 4 hours.

- Take the chicken away from the marinade, then add marinade to a large skillet on medium-high heat. Slice chicken breasts in half on vertical and use a meat mallet to quickly pound each piece to 1/2 inch thickness. Arrange a slice of cheese, a slice of ham, and a sprinkle of brown sugar on each piece. Roll them and use toothpicks to secure, brown in the skillet of marinate.

- Set an oven to 165°C (325°F) and start preheating.

- Arrange the browned rollups in a 9x13 inch baking dish, add a little marinade to the chicken and save at least 3 tablespoons in the skillet. Dust pepper and salt over the chicken to taste, plus a little brown sugar.

- In the prepared oven, bake chicken rollups until juices from the chicken run clear and the chicken is cooked through, half an hour.

- To make the sauce: At the same time, put the flour into the skillet of the saved marinade. Pour in 2 cups of wine, constantly stirring and allowing the sauce to thicken. Stir in horseradish, a little brown sugar, honey, and mustard. Add pepper and salt to flavor to taste, then heat through and serve alongside chicken rollups.

Nutrition Information

- Calories: 405 calories;
- Total Fat: 15.5

- Sodium: 656
- Total Carbohydrate: 17.1
- Cholesterol: 75
- Protein: 26.2

Cornish Game Hens With Garlic And Rosemary

Serving: 4

Ingredients

- 3 tablespoons olive oil

- 24 cloves garlic

- 1/3 cup white wine

- 1/3 cup low-sodium chicken broth

- 4 Cornish game hens

- salt and pepper to taste

- 1 lemon, quartered

- 4 sprigs fresh rosemary

- 4 sprigs fresh rosemary, for garnish

Direction

- Preheat the oven to 230 degrees C/450 degrees F.
- Use 1 tbsp. olive oil to rub hens. Season hens lightly with pepper and salt. Put 1 sprig rosemary and 1 lemon wedge in every hen's cavity. Put in a big heavy roasting pan. Surround hens with garlic cloves. Roast for 25 minutes in the preheated oven.
- Lower the oven temperature to 175 degrees C/350 degrees F. Whisk together leftover 2 tbsp. oil, chicken broth and wine in a mixing bowl. Pour on hens. Keep roasting for about 25 minutes longer until hens become golden brown and the juices are clear. Baste using the pan juices in 10- minute intervals.
- Put hens on a platter, putting any cavity juices in the roasting pan. Use aluminum foil to tent hens to retain warmth. Put garlic cloves and pan juices in a medium saucepan. Boil for about 6 minutes until liquid is reduce to become a sauce consistency. Cut hens lengthwise in half. Put on plates. Put garlic and sauce around the hens. Top with rosemary sprigs. Serve.

Nutrition Information

- Calories: 814 calories;
- Total Fat: 57.5
- Sodium: 1383
- Total Carbohydrate: 9.7
- Cholesterol: 340
- Protein: 59.4

Cornish Hens The Easy Way

Serving: 4

Ingredients

- 1/4 teaspoon ground cumin
- kosher salt to taste
- ground black pepper to taste
- 4 Cornish game hens
- 2 limes, halved
- 2 teaspoons olive oil
- 1/4 teaspoon chili powder

Direction

- Turn the oven to 425°F (220°C) to preheat.
- Rub a lime half over each hen. Drizzle olive oil over the hens and use pepper, kosher salt, cumin and chili powder to season. On a rack in a shallow roasting pan, put the hens.

- In the preheated oven, roast the hens for 15 minutes. Lower the heat to 350°F (175°C) and keep roasting until the internal temperature is 180°F (80°C), or about 30 minutes.

Nutrition Information

- Calories: 332 calories;

- Sodium: 556

- Total Carbohydrate: 3.8

- Cholesterol: 151

- Protein: 26

- Total Fat: 23.5

Crab Croissants

Ingredients

- 1 cup minced onion

- 2 cloves garlic

- 1 large tomato, diced

- salt and pepper to taste

- 12 ounces cooked and flaked blue crabmeat

- 2/3 cup blue cheese salad dressing

- 1/3 cup mayonnaise

- 1 cup seasoned dry bread crumbs

- 1/2 cup grated Asiago cheese

- 6 plain croissants, split in half

Direction

- Mix garlic, mayonnaise, onion, crabmeat, bread crumbs, and blue cheese dressing in a medium bowl. Stir in tomato, pepper, and salt to add some flavor. Fold in Asiago cheese, or you can sprinkle it on top before serving.

- Spread a half cup of the mixture into half of each croissant, and place the other halves on top.

Nutrition Information

- Calories: 667 calories;
- Total Carbohydrate: 45.5
- Cholesterol: 124
- Protein: 23.9
- Total Fat: 42
- Sodium: 1221

Crab Stuffed Lobster Tail

Serving: 2

Ingredients

- 1/4 teaspoon salt, or to taste
- 1/4 teaspoon freshly ground white pepper, or to taste
- 15 buttery round crackers, crushed
- 1/2 cup jumbo lump crabmeat
- 1/4 cup clarified butter
- 1 tablespoon chopped fresh parsley leaves
- 2 lobster tails, split along the center top
- 2 teaspoons butter, melted
- 1 tablespoon fresh lemon juice
- 1 teaspoon seafood seasoning (such as Old Bay®)
- 1 clove garlic, minced
- 1 teaspoon lemon zest

Direction

- Preheat the oven to 220°C or 425°F.

- Pull apart the edges of the split lobster shells and delicately lift the tail meat until it rests on top of the shells. Put the prepared lobster tails on a baking sheet.
- Use a teaspoon of melted butter to brush each section of the tail meat.
- In a bowl, gently mix together white pepper, crushed crackers, salt, crabmeat, lemon juice, one quarter cup clarified butter, lemon zest, parsley, garlic, and seafood seasoning until well combined.
- Scoop half of the mixture on each lobster tail, press gently and shape it lightly to avoid the stuffing from falling off.
- Bake for 10-12 minutes until the stuffing is golden and the meat is non-transparent. An inserted instant-read thermometer in the thickest lobster tail part should register 65°C or 145°F.

Nutrition Information

- Calories: 596 calories;
- Protein: 35.9
- Total Fat: 41.4

- Sodium: 1483
- Total Carbohydrate: 19.4
- Cholesterol: 203

Cracked Black Venison

Serving: 4

Ingredients

- 2 (1/2 pound) venison steaks
- 2 teaspoons cracked black pepper
- 2 teaspoons coarse salt
- 1 tablespoon unsalted butter

Direction

- Season venison steaks with salt and pepper. In small saucepan, melt butter on low heat; skin solids off, the milk substance that appears; discard. Put butter in big skillet; heat on high heat.
- Sauté the venison steaks in skillet, 3 minutes per side. Lower heat to medium. Cook, 15 minutes per side for medium and 10 minutes per side for rare. Take off heat. Before slicing to long strips, let stand for 2-3 minutes. Immediately serve.

Nutrition Information

- Calories: 151 calories;
- Cholesterol: 93
- Protein: 23.3
- Total Fat: 5.6
- Sodium: 925
- Total Carbohydrate: 0.7

Creamy Chicken Marsala Fettuccine

Serving: 4

Ingredients

- 1/4 teaspoon paprika
- 1/4 teaspoon cayenne pepper
- salt and freshly ground black pepper (optional)
- 1 cup chicken broth
- 2 tablespoons chopped fresh flat-leaf parsley
- 2 tablespoons olive oil
- 2 tablespoons butter, divided
- 1 sweet onion, chopped
- 1 cup shiitake mushrooms, cut in half
- 1 cup fresh oyster mushrooms, cut in half
- 1 cup cremini mushrooms, cut in half
- 1 (12 ounce) package dry fettuccine pasta
- 2 tablespoons butter
- 2 tablespoons minced garlic
- 3/4 cup Marsala wine

- 1 (8 ounce) container mascarpone cheese
- 2 tablespoons Dijon mustard
- 4 skinless, boneless chicken breast halves
- 1/2 cup all-purpose flour

Direction

- Arrange chicken breasts between two sheets of the heavy plastic (resealable freezer bags could also do the trick well) onto a solid and flat surface. Use smooth side of the meat mallet to pound the chicken firmly to a thickness that is roughly a quarter in. In a shallow bowl, stir black pepper, salt, cayenne pepper, paprika and flour. Press each of the chicken breasts to flour mixture on both of the sides. Tap off the excess flour.

- Heat the olive oil and 1 tbsp. of butter on medium heat in a skillet till butter gives off a lightly toasted fragrance, and pan-fry chicken for roughly 3 minutes on each side till turning brown on both of the sides. Put them aside. Melt 1 additional tbsp. of butter in the skillet, and cook and whisk onion for roughly 5 minutes till becoming translucent; whisk in garlic, cremini mushrooms, oyster mushrooms and shiitake mushrooms, and cook for 10-12 minutes till mushrooms give off the juice and start to become browned.

- Fill a big pot with lightly-salted water and heat to a rolling boil on high heat. When water is boiling, whisk in fettuccini, and bring back to a boil. Cook pasta, without covering, whisk once in a while, for roughly 8 minutes till pasta becomes thoroughly cooked but still firm to bite. Drain them well in a colander that is placed in the sink. Arrange pasta to a serving dish, and toss along with 2 tbsp. of butter; use black pepper and salt to season to taste, and keep them warm.

- After mushroom juices have evaporated, add the Marsala wine to the sauce, and scrape up and dissolve any browned flavor bits in skillet's bottom. Switch the heat to high, and whisk for roughly 3 minutes till 1/2 of the wine is evaporated; whisk in the chicken broth, Dijon mustard and mascarpone; cook, whisk continuously, for 3 more minutes till sauce becomes thick slightly. Lower the heat to medium low; bring back cooked chicken breasts to the sauce. Cook for roughly 5 minutes till sauce becomes thick and chicken juices run clear. Whisk in the parsley. Serve along with the buttered fettuccine.

Nutrition Information

- Calories: 1028 calories;
- Total Fat: 49.4
- Sodium: 391
- Total Carbohydrate: 90.8
- Cholesterol: 168
- Protein: 44.9

Creamy Saffron Shrimp With Gnocchi And Caramelized Onion

Serving: 4

Ingredients

- 1 teaspoon brown sugar
- 1 (16 ounce) package potato gnocchi
- 20 peeled and deveined large shrimp (21 to 30 per pound)
- 3 tablespoons reduced-fat sour cream
- 1 tablespoon butter
- 1 large onion, thinly sliced
- 6 mushrooms, sliced
- 1 teaspoon paprika
- 1 pinch saffron
- salt to taste
- 2 tablespoons shredded fresh basil
- 1/4 cup grated Parmesan cheese

Direction

- In a large skillet, melt the butter on medium heat. Stir in brown sugar, mushrooms, and onion. Stir and cook for 10 minutes until the onions are cooked to a deep brown color. Take the caramelized onions out and put aside.

- Bring a large pot of lightly salted water to a rolling boil on high heat. Add the gnocchi and stir once the water is boiling, then boil again. Cook for 3 minutes until the gnocchi rises to the surface; drain the gnocchi and keep it warm.

- Arrange the skillet on medium-high heat, add shrimp and stir. Stir and cook for 5 minutes until the shrimp are not translucent in the center anymore and the outside turns pink. Add saffron, paprika, sour cream, and caramelized onions. Stir and cook until the mixture starts to simmer, then fold in the cooked gnocchi gently and flavor with salt to taste.

- To serve, fill a serving dish with the gnocchi and dust with Parmesan cheese and shredded basil.

Nutrition Information

- Calories: 333 calories;

- Cholesterol: 198

- Protein: 23.7

- Total Fat: 14.7

- Sodium: 374

- Total Carbohydrate: 26.7

Crispy Chinese Noodles With Eggplant And Peanuts

Serving: 4

Ingredients

- 1/4 cup red wine vinegar
- 1/3 cup water
- 1 tablespoon minced fresh ginger root
- 1 tablespoon white sugar
- 4 tablespoons chopped, unsalted dry-roasted peanuts
- 1 tablespoon chopped fresh mint (optional)
- 2 tablespoons vegetarian fish sauce
- 2 cups sliced onion
- 1 medium eggplant, cubed
- 1 teaspoon salt
- 16 ounces fresh Chinese wheat noodles
- 2 tablespoons sherry

- 1 tablespoon cornstarch
- 3 tablespoons canola oil
- 4 cloves garlic, minced
- 1 red bell pepper, julienned

Direction

- Put cubed eggplants in a colander. Drizzle with salt then toss adequately. Drain the eggplant for 15 minutes then wash off lightly with water. Drain the eggplants again in the colander.
- Boil water in a large pot then add the noodles and boil them in the water until they're tender, about 5 minutes. Drain the noodles and wash off properly with cold water. Let the noodles drain in the colander for at least 10 minutes.
- Mix together the sherry and the cornstarch in a small bowl. Blend adequately then set it aside.
- Mix together the red wine vinegar, water, ginger, imitation fish sauce, sugar, and onions in a cooking pan. Bring to a boil then lower the heat to low and allow the mixture to simmer for 5 minutes.
- Heat 1 1/2 tablespoon of oil over medium-high heat in a large cooking pan that is preferably non-stick.

Cook the eggplant in the oil for 5 minutes with frequent stirring. Mix in the red pepper and garlic and cook for 5 minutes while stirring occasionally, until the eggplant has softened. Pour in the onion-vinegar mixture as well as the cornstarch-sherry mixture then let cook for 2-3 minutes more with occasional stirring. Make sure to keep this mixture warm.

- Heat the remaining 1 1/2 tablespoons oil in a large non-stick pan over medium-high heat just until the oil starts to smoke. Add the noodles then put 2-3 plates on top of the noodles so to brown more of the surface. Allow the noodles to sit for 5 minutes over medium-high heat. Take off the plates when the noodles have already formed a golden brown crust on its underside. Turn them over using a spatula then cook for 5 minutes on the other side. Turn the heat off.

- Mix the peanuts into the eggplant mixture then spoon them onto individual plates. Separate noodles into 4 parts. Place the noodles on top of the sauce and vegetables. If you prefer, drizzle with mint then serve.

Nutrition Information

- Calories: 558 calories;
- Total Carbohydrate: 88.2
- Cholesterol: 0
- Protein: 12.3
- Total Fat: 16.9
- Sodium: 1310

Cuban Pork Roast II

Serving: 8

Ingredients

- 5 pounds boneless loin pork roast
- 6 cloves crushed garlic
- 1/2 teaspoon dried rosemary, crushed
- 1/2 teaspoon dried dill weed
- 1/2 teaspoon dried oregano
- 1 cup dry red wine
- 10 cloves garlic

Direction

- In a small bowl, combine red wine, oregano, dill, rosemary and crushed garlic together. Put the roast into a large glass or plastic container; pour the wine mixture over the meat; cover. Marinate in the refrigerator for overnight.
- Set the oven at 325°F (165°C) and start preheating.

- Transfer the meat into a Dutch oven. Using a sharp knife, create eight to ten 1-in.-deep cuts into the meat. Into each hole, insert a whole peeled garlic clove. Pour the marinade over the meat; cover.
- Roast till an instant-read thermometer reads 145°F (63°C) when inserted into the center of the roast, 35 minutes per pound.

Nutrition Information

- Calories: 633 calories;
- Sodium: 121
- Total Carbohydrate: 2.9
- Cholesterol: 170
- Protein: 56.8
- Total Fat: 39.8

Cuban Shredded Pork

Serving: 5

Ingredients

- 8 black peppercorns
- 1 tablespoon garlic powder, or to taste
- 1 tablespoon onion powder
- salt to taste
- 1 1/2 pounds boneless pork chops
- 1 pint water to cover
- 1 lime, juiced
- 1 sprig fresh thyme
- 2 tablespoons olive oil
- 1 large onion, halved and thinly sliced
- 3 cloves garlic, peeled and sliced
- 1 lime, juiced
-
- 1/4 cup chopped fresh cilantro

Direction

- Mix garlic powder, water, thyme sprig, juice of one lime, salt, peppercorns, and onion powder in a large saucepan. Heat the mixture to a boil. Place in pork chops, decrease the heat to medium-low and let to simmer for about 1 to 1 1/2 hours until the meat becomes very tender. Pour in extra water as needed to keep the chops covered.

- Switch off the heat and allow the chops sit in the broth for half an hour. Take out the chops from the broth and shred while removing the excess fat. Reserve.

- Over medium-high heat, heat olive oil in a large frying pan, add the shredded pork and then fry for about 5 minutes until it's almost crisp. Add the garlic and onion and continue to cook for about 10 minutes until onion is just tender but slightly crisp. Pour in the juice of one lime, combine well and then mix with cilantro. Serve.

Nutrition Information

- Calories: 202 calories;
- Total Fat: 10.7
- Sodium: 103
- Total Carbohydrate: 8.1
- Cholesterol: 43
- Protein: 18.5

Deviled Crab

Serving: 8

Ingredients

- 1 cup dry bread crumbs
- 1 1/2 tablespoons fresh lemon juice
- 1/4 cup fresh parsley, minced
- 1 1/2 tablespoons fresh basil, minced
- 4 tablespoons vegetable oil
- 1 tablespoon vegetable oil
- 1 tablespoon butter
- 1 cup all-purpose flour
- 2 cloves garlic, minced
- 2 cups clam juice
- 1/2 cup white wine
- 1/8 teaspoon freshly ground black pepper
- 1/8 teaspoon crushed red pepper flakes
- 1/2 cup heavy cream
- 1 3/4 pounds crabmeat
- 1/8 teaspoon salt

- 3/4 teaspoon Worcestershire sauce
- 3/4 teaspoon hot pepper sauce

Direction

- Put hot pepper sauce, Worcestershire sauce, salt and crabmeat in mixing bowl. Stir well.
- Form mixture of crab to cakes; roll into bread crumbs.
- Heat four tablespoons oil in medium-size skillet on moderate heat. Sauté cakes, for approximately 5 minutes. Flip; let cook till golden brown, or for 5 minutes more.
- Sauce: Heat a tablespoon each of butter and oil in a 1 1/2-quart saucepan. Put flour into oil slowly, mixing continuously. Cook, about 5 minutes.
- Put in clam juice slowly, mixing vigorously and continuously. Add black pepper, crushed red pepper flakes and white wine. Let simmer. Put in parsley, basil and cream. Allow to simmer yet do not let boil. Once mixture thickens enough to coat back of spoon evenly, it is done.
- Top crab cakes with sauce to serve.

Nutrition Information

- Calories: 380 calories;

- Cholesterol: 103

- Protein: 26.3

- Total Fat: 18

- Sodium: 675

- Total Carbohydrate: 24.3

Dill Poached Salmon

Serving: 4

Ingredients

- 1 bunch fresh dill tied with kitchen twine

- 4 (4 ounce) fillets salmon

- 2 cups chicken stock

Direction

- In a large pot, put salmon fillets, and then add in chicken stock. Heat to boil, decrease the heat to low and add dill into the pot. Cover the pot and let to cook for about 15 minutes or until the fish flakes easily with a fork.

Nutrition Information

- Calories: 219 calories;

- Total Fat: 10.9

- Sodium: 405

- Total Carbohydrate: 1

- Cholesterol: 74

- Protein: 25.8

Dry Brined Smoked Salmon

Serving: 12

Ingredients

- 2 (12 fluid ounce) cans or bottles cola-flavored carbonated beverage (such as Coca-Cola®) (optional)

- 1 1/2 cups brown sugar, divided

- 1 cup kosher salt

- 3 pounds salmon fillets

- 1/2 cup honey

- 3 cups wood chips, soaked

Direction

- In a small bowl, mix the kosher salt and a cup of brown sugar.

- At the bottom of the 9-inch baking pan, spread the brown sugar mixture in a thin layer and top

67

it with 2-3 salmon fillets. Cover the fillets with some of the brown sugar mixture. Continue layering until the salmon fillets are completely coated. Use a plastic wrap to cover the pan. Refrigerate it for 8 hours or up to overnight.

- Follow the manufacturer's instructions to set the smoker to 195°F (91°C) for preheating.

- Wash the salmon fillets to remove the brown sugar mixture. Lightly brush honey all over the fillets. Sprinkle the top with the remaining 1/2 cup of brown sugar.

- Fill the smoker's water pan with a cola-flavored beverage. Pour in water, filling it up to 1-inch of the top. Arrange half of the wood chips around the perimeter of the hot charcoal. Position the salmon onto the cooking racks.

- Cook the salmon for 2 hours, adding extra wood chips if necessary until the inserted instant-read thermometer in the center registers 145°F (63°C). Allow it to cool for at least 15 minutes before serving.

Nutrition Information

- Calories: 296 calories;

- Cholesterol: 49

- Protein: 20.8

- Total Fat: 3.8

- Sodium: 7653

- Total Carbohydrate: 45.1

Duck Breasts With Raspberry Sauce

Serving: 4

Ingredients

- 1/2 cup red wine

- 1/4 cup creme de cassis liqueur

- 1 teaspoon cornstarch

- 4 ounces raspberries

- 4 duck breast halves

- 2 teaspoons sea salt

- 2 teaspoons ground cinnamon

- 4 teaspoons demerara sugar

Direction

- Pre-heat the oven to a broiler setting. Score the duck breasts using a fork through the skin; be sure not to penetrate all the way to the meat.

- Heat up a large heavy skillet over medium high heat, and then place the duck breasts in skin-side down to fry. Cook for 10 minutes, or until the fat runs out and the skin turns brown. Take the breasts out of the pan, pour out most of the fat, and then return the breasts to the pan. Fry skin-side up for another 10 minutes before completely removing duck breasts from the skillet. Set them aside to rest on a baking sheet. Mix cinnamon and Demerera sugar with sea salt and pour over the duck skin breasts. Pour most of the fat out of the frying pan.

- In a small bowl, mix cassis and cornstarch with red wine. Simmer it in the skillet for about 3 minutes, continuously stirring until the sauce has thickened. Then add raspberries and let simmer for another 1 minute until thoroughly heated.

- Broil the duck breasts, skin-side up, for a minute, or until the sugar mixture begins to caramelize. Thinly slice the duck breasts, partner with a little sauce over the top, and serve warm.

Nutrition Information

- Calories: 116 calories;
- Protein: 0.3
- Total Fat: 0.2
- Sodium: 883
- Total Carbohydrate: 15.2
- Cholesterol: 0

Duck Cassoulet

Serving: 8

Ingredients

- 1 sprig fresh thyme

- 1/2 pound bacon

- 1 sprig fresh rosemary

- 1 pound dry navy beans, soaked overnight

- 1 bay leaf

- 1 pound pork sausage links, sliced

- 1 tablespoon whole cloves

- 1 whole onion, peeled

- 3 sprigs fresh parsley

- 3 carrots, peeled and sliced

- 3 cloves garlic, minced

- 1 pound skinned, boned duck breast halves, sliced into thin strips.

- 1 fresh tomato, chopped

Direction

- Brown the sliced sausage on medium heat in a big skillet

- Insert whole cloves inside the onion. Roll up the bacon then tie it using a string. Tie the rosemary, parsley, and thyme together.

- Put duck, minced garlic, carrots, bay leaf, fresh herbs, onion studded with cloves, bacon, sausage and soaked beans in a big slow cooker. Pour sufficient amount of water to cover the other ingredients. On high setting, cook for 1 hour. Adjust heat to low, keep on cooking for 6-8 hours.

- Get rid of the herbs, bacon and onion. Mix in the chopped tomatoes. Keep cooking for 30 minutes. Serve

Nutrition Information

- Calories: 548 calories;

- Total Fat: 26.8

- Sodium: 584

- Total Carbohydrate: 40.2

- Cholesterol: 104

- Protein: 36.7

Easy Chicken Korma

Serving: 4

Ingredients

- 3 tablespoons olive oil
- 4 boneless skinless chicken breast halves, chopped
- 1/3 cup sliced almonds
- 2 large onions, chopped
- 6 tablespoons plain yogurt
- 2 tablespoons mango chutney
- 4 cloves garlic, minced
- 2 teaspoons turmeric powder
- 3 tablespoons butter
- 2 teaspoons garam masala
- 2 teaspoons salt
- 1 teaspoon red chile powder

Direction

- Turn oven to 350°F (175°C) to preheat. Lightly oil a 2-qt. baking dish.

- In a skillet, heat butter and oil over medium heat. Add onions and cook until soft.

- In the bowl of a food processor, place garam masala, chili powder, turmeric, garlic, mango chutney, yogurt, and onion. Blend the mixture to make a smooth sauce; the consistency should be about of thick cream. Add little water or yogurt to thin sauce if necessary. Distribute chicken into the greased baking dish, and pour the onion sauce over.

- Bake for 30 minutes in the preheated oven, or until thoroughly cooked. Garnish with sliced almonds on top, and enjoy.

Nutrition Information

- Calories: 423 calories;

- Total Fat: 25.9

- Sodium: 1412

- Total Carbohydrate: 16.7

- Cholesterol: 93

- Protein: 31.5

Easy Prime Rib Roast

Ingredients

- 1 pinch finely ground dried thyme

- salt and ground black pepper to taste

- 1 (4.5 pound) bone-in prime rib roast

- 4 cloves garlic, finely chopped, or more to taste

- 1/4 teaspoon dried rosemary, or more to taste

- 1 pinch crushed dried sage

- 1/4 cup Worcestershire sauce, or more to taste

- 1/4 cup soy sauce, or more to taste

Direction

- In a small bowl, combine the sage, pepper, garlic, salt, thyme and rosemary together. Coat the roast all over with the garlic mixture. Cut a slit in the middle of the roast parallel to the bones. In a plastic oven bag, put in the seasoned roast, soy sauce and Worcestershire sauce, focusing on the slit on the roast. Tie the oven bag and let it marinate in the fridge for not less than 2 hours, flip the roast from time to time to marinate evenly on every side.

- Take the roast out of the fridge and let it sit for 1-2 hours until it gets to room temperature. Take the marinated roast from the oven bag and throw away the marinade mixture. In a roasting pan, put the marinated roast with the fat side facing up.

- Preheat the oven to 500°F (260°C).

- Put in preheated oven and bake for 15 minutes. Reduce the heat to 350°F (175°C) and keep cooking for about 1 hour until a thermometer inserted on the meat indicates 145°F (65°C). Allow the baked roast to rest for 20 minutes before cutting.

Nutrition Information

- Calories: 340 calories;

- Cholesterol: 90

- Protein: 31

- Total Fat: 21.8

- Sodium: 637

- Total Carbohydrate: 2.9

Eggless Pasta

Serving: 4

Ingredients

- 2 cups semolina flour
- 1/2 teaspoon salt
- 1/2 cup warm water

Direction

- Mix salt and flour in a big bowl. Add warm water; mix to create stiff dough. If dough looks dry, increase water.

- Pat dough to ball; turn onto lightly floured surface and knead for 10-15 minutes then cover. Rest dough for 20 minutes.

- Using pasta machine/rolling pin, roll out dough; work using 1/4 dough at 1 time. To keep from drying out, keep others covered. Roll to

1/16-in. thick by hand. By machine, stop on third to final setting.

- Cut pasta to preferred shapes.

- Cook fresh noodles for 3-5 minutes in boiling salted water; drain.

Nutrition Information

- Calories: 301 calories;
- Total Carbohydrate: 60.8
- Cholesterol: 0
- Protein: 10.6
- Total Fat: 0.9
- Sodium: 292

Eggs Benedict With Salmon

Serving: 8

Ingredients

- 3/4 cup plain low-fat yogurt
- 8 slices rye bread
- 8 ounces smoked salmon, cut into thin slices
- 1 tablespoon chopped fresh parsley, for garnish
- 1 teaspoon capers, for garnish
- 2 teaspoons lemon juice
- 3 egg yolks
- 1/2 teaspoon prepared Dijon-style mustard
- 1/4 teaspoon salt
- 1/4 teaspoon white sugar
- 1 pinch ground black pepper
- 1 dash hot pepper sauce
- 8 eggs

Direction

- For the sauce: whip hot sauce, pepper, sugar, salt, mustard, egg yolks, lemon juice and yogurt together in the top of a double boiler. Put it over the simmering water and cook while stirring continuously for 6-8 minutes or until the sauce is thick enough that you can coat the back of a spoon with the sauce.

- Heat to a boil 2 quarts of salted water in a big stock pot. Break 1 egg at a time carefully into the boiling water. After adding all the eggs, lower the heat to medium. Use a slotted spoon to take the eggs out when they float to the top, let them drain briefly.

- For final dish assembling: Toast slices of bread and arrange on warm plates. Put a hot poached egg and a slice of smoked salmon on top of each toast piece. Sprinkle yogurt sauce over, decorate with capers and parsley.

Nutrition Information

- Calories: 223 calories;

- Total Fat: 9.3

- Sodium: 617

- Total Carbohydrate: 18.1

- Cholesterol: 271

- Protein: 16.4

Erin's Indonesian Chicken

Serving: 4

Ingredients

- 1 cup uncooked long grain white rice
- 2 cups water
- 1 pound fresh green beans, trimmed and snapped
- 2 teaspoons olive oil
- 1 pound skinless, boneless chicken breast halves - cut into chunks
- 3/4 cup low-sodium chicken broth
- 1/3 cup smooth peanut butter
- 2 teaspoons honey
- 1 tablespoon low sodium soy sauce
- 1 teaspoon red chile paste
- 2 tablespoons lemon juice
- 3 green onions, thinly sliced
- 2 tablespoons chopped peanuts (optional)

Direction

- Boil water and rice in a pot. Lower the heat to low, covered, and let it simmer for 20 minutes.
- Add the green beans into the pot that is fitted with one steamer basket over the boiling water, and let it steam till turning soft but crisp or for 10 minutes.
- Heat oil in a skillet, and cook chicken till the juices run clear or for 5 minutes per side.
- In a saucepan, combine lemon juice, chile paste, soy sauce, honey, peanut butter and chicken broth on medium heat. Cook and whisk till becoming thick slightly for 5 minutes. Stir in green beans. Serve on the rice. Use the peanuts and green onions to decorate.

Nutrition Information

- Calories: 530 calories;
- Total Fat: 18.6
- Sodium: 322
- Total Carbohydrate: 58.1
- Cholesterol: 59
- Protein: 35.4

Father In Law's Scallops With Sun Dried Tomatoes And Bacon

Serving: 4 | Prep: 20mins | Cook: 20mins | Ready in:

Ingredients

- 1/4 cup heavy cream
- 2 tablespoons butter, at room temperature
- 2 teaspoons minced garlic
- 4 slices double smoked bacon
- 1 1/2 tablespoons olive oil
- 12 large scallops, patted dry
- 1/2 cup dry white wine
- 3 tablespoons sun-dried tomatoes packed in oil, drained and thinly sliced
- 1 (8 ounce) package angel hair pasta
- salt and black pepper to taste

Direction

- Place a large deep skillet on medium high heat then put the bacon and cook for about 10 minutes, regularly turning, until browned equally. Use a paper towel lined plate to drain the bacon slices. Slice the bacon and reserve.
- Place water that is lightly salted in a large pot and make it boil for the pasta. While water is coming to a boil, heat oil in a large heavy skillet on high heat and put in the scallops to fry for about two minutes per side until opaque and brown in color. Remove scallops and put on a plate.
- Add in the angel hair pasta into the boiling water, and boil again. Cook the pasta for 4 to 5 minutes without cover regularly stirring, until the pasta has cooked through but remain firm to bite. Strain well in a colander set in the sink, and split between four plates the hot pasta.
- In a skillet, place the sun-dried tomatoes and white wine, and get rid of and melt any browned flavor bits left in the pan. Mix in the cream, make it boil

over medium heat, lower the heat, and simmer for about two minutes until becomes thick. Get the pan from the heat, and stir in the garlic and butter. Mix the butter into the sauce, put back the scallops to the pan, then cover with the sauce.

- Put scallops and sauce on top of the pasta, drizzle with chopped bacon, and use pepper and salt to taste.

Nutrition Information

- Calories: 520 calories;
- Sodium: 601
- Total Carbohydrate: 36.8
- Cholesterol: 83
- Protein: 29.1
- Total Fat: 26

Fennel Risotto

Serving: 6 |

Ingredients

- 4 bulbs fennel
- 1 tablespoon butter
- 1 medium onion, chopped
- 2 cups uncooked Arborio rice
- 7 cups vegetable broth
- 1 cup heavy cream
- 6 tablespoons freshly grated Parmesan cheese
- 1 tablespoon dried parsley
- freshly ground black pepper to taste

Direction

- Cut off the base of the fennel bulbs. Remove its core by cutting a cone shape into the base. Cut the fennel vertically or lengthwise, and then cut it into 1/4-inch thick slices.
- Place the butter in a heavy-bottomed stock pot and melt it over medium heat. Cook the fennel and

onions in butter for 2 minutes. Mix in rice. Cook the mixture for 2 more minutes, stirring continuously until toasted lightly. Mix in a cup of vegetable broth. Keep stirring the mixture until the liquid is almost absorbed completely. Do the same process with the remaining broth while stirring the mixture continuously. Take note that mixing the broth should take a total of 15-20 minutes.

- Mix in parsley, 3 tbsp. of Parmesan, and cream. Cook the mixture until the risotto is creamy and thick and the rice is done. Season the mixture with black pepper to taste. Distribute the risotto among the 6 bowls. Sprinkle each with the remaining cheese.

Nutrition Information

- Calories: 537 calories;
- Total Fat: 19
- Sodium: 725
- Total Carbohydrate: 81.3
- Cholesterol: 64
- Protein: 11.2

Feta And Olive Meatballs

Serving: 8

Ingredients

- 1 pound ground lamb
- 1/2 cup chopped green olives
- 2 eggs
- 1 teaspoon Italian seasoning
- 1/2 cup chopped fresh parsley
- 2 tablespoons finely chopped onion
- 1/2 cup crumbled feta cheese

Direction

- Preheat oven broiler.

- Mix Italian seasoning, eggs, green olives, feta cheese, onion, parsley and ground lamb in a big bowl; form to 16 meatballs. Put onto baking sheet, 2-in. apart.

- Broil 3-in. from heat till browned on top. Flip; broil other side.

Nutrition Information

- Calories: 185 calories;
- Total Fat: 13.7
- Sodium: 482
- Total Carbohydrate: 1.5
- Cholesterol: 98
- Protein: 13.8

Fettuccine In Creamy Mushroom And Sage Sauce

Serving: 2

Ingredients

- 1 shallot, chopped
- 1 clove garlic, chopped
- 4 ounces chopped fresh oyster mushrooms
- 1/2 cup heavy cream
- 8 ounces spinach fettuccine pasta
- 1 tablespoon extra virgin olive oil
- 1 tablespoon chopped fresh sage
- salt and pepper to taste

Direction

- Boil a big pot of slightly salted water. Put in the pasta and cook till al dente or for 8 to 10 minutes; drain.

- In a medium saucepan, heat the olive oil over medium heat, and cook garlic and shallots till clear. Mix in the mushrooms, and cook till soft. Stir in sage and heavy cream. Cook and mix till thickened.
- Toss cooked fettucine and sauce together, and add pepper and salt to season and serve.

Nutrition Information

- Calories: 612 calories;
- Cholesterol: 82
- Protein: 16.5
- Total Fat: 31.4
- Sodium: 289
- Total Carbohydrate: 70.2

Filipino Ribs

Serving: 11

Ingredients

- 1/2 cup honey

- 2 tablespoons brown sugar

- 1 tablespoon Worcestershire sauce

- 2 medium onions, cut into wedges

- 1 medium onion, finely chopped

- 6 pounds pork spareribs

- 1 tablespoon grated fresh ginger

- 6 tablespoons soy sauce

- 1/4 teaspoon ground black pepper

- 6 whole star anise pods

- 1 tablespoon vegetable oil

- 1 tablespoon lemon juice

Direction

- In a 5- to 6-qt.stock pot, put the ribs with star anise, pepper, 4 tablespoons of the soy sauce, and 2 wedges onions. Make it boil. Lower heat to medium low, cover and allow to simmer in meat juice for approximately 1 1/4 hours, until the ribs are tender once pierced. Whisk occasionally.

- In the meantime, in a medium skillet set on medium heat, add oil. Stir-fry the rest of the chopped onion, whisking often, until onions turns soft. Mix in the rest of 2 tablespoons of soy sauce, lemon juice, Worcestershire sauce, sugar, honey, and ginger. Cook everything, whisking, until well combined. Separate from heat.

- Prepare the oven by preheating to 400°F (200°C).

- Take the ribs from the stock pot using tongs then pile in one layer in an 11x6-inch baking dish. Apply honey mixture to equally brush and place in the preheated oven and bake for approximately 30 minutes, basting often with pan drippings, until ribs are well glazed.

Nutrition Information

- Calories: 773 calories;

- Total Fat: 59.3

- Sodium: 710

- Total Carbohydrate: 19.4

- Cholesterol: 198

- Protein: 39.3

Fish Baked En Croute De Sel (Fish Baked In A Salt Crust)

Serving: 4

Ingredients

- 2 sprigs fresh cilantro, or more to taste

- 2 sprigs fresh parsley, or more to taste

- 2 pounds salt

- 7 bay leaves

- 2 pounds whole rainbow trout, gutted and cleaned, heads and tails still on

- 2 sprigs fresh dill, or more to taste

Direction

- Preheat the oven to 200 degrees C/400 degrees F. Line aluminum foil on a baking sheet.

- Spread 1/4 - 1/2-lb. salt on aluminum foil to around the same shape as the fish. Put bay leaves on salt. Put fish on top. Stuff dill, parsley and cilantro into fish cavity. Firmly pack down leftover salt on fish. Leave tail and head exposed.

- Bake in preheated oven for 30 minutes until salt crust becomes golden.

- Remove fish from oven. Crack open salt crust carefully. Remove the top. Peel off fish skin to expose flesh. Use a spatula/fish knife to lift top fillet off the bones. In one piece, remove bones by lifting from the tail then pull upwards towards the head. Lift bottom fillet out with a spatula/knife.

Nutrition Information

- Calories: 272 calories;

- Cholesterol: 122

- Protein: 41.1

- Total Fat: 10.5

- Sodium: 88088

- Total Carbohydrate: 1.1

Fish Roll Ups

Ingredients

- 2 tablespoons minced fresh parsley
- 1/4 teaspoon garlic powder, or to taste
- 2 tablespoons lemon juice
- 1/4 cup grated Parmesan cheese
- 3 tablespoons butter
- salt and pepper to taste
- 24 buttery round crackers, crushed
- 12 (6 ounce) fillets sole
- 2/3 cup butter
- 2 tablespoons minced onion
- 1 cup minced crabmeat

Direction

- Prepare the oven by preheating to 375°F (190°C). Prepare a 9x13-inch baking pan lightly coated with cooking spray.

- Melt the butter in frying pan set over medium heat. Add onion and stir-fry for 1 minute. Mix in pepper, garlic powder, salt, parsley, and crabmeat and cook for 1 more minute. Take away from heat and mix in crushed crackers.

- Spread mixture over filets; sprinkle with Parmesan cheese and lemon juice. Roll up filets, using toothpicks to seal and transfer to prepared baking dish. Drizzle each roll with butter and use foil to cover the pan tightly.

- Bake for 15-17 minutes in the preheated oven until fish flakes.

Nutrition Information

- Calories: 323 calories;

- Total Fat: 17.7

- Sodium: 341

- Total Carbohydrate: 4.7

- Cholesterol: 126

- Protein: 34.7

Foolproof Rib Roast

Serving: 6

Ingredients

- 1 teaspoon ground black pepper

- 1 teaspoon garlic powder

- 1 (5 pound) standing beef rib roast

- 2 teaspoons salt

Direction

- Let the roast sit in room temperature for not less than 1 hour.

- Preheat your oven to 375°F (190°C). In a small cup, mix the pepper, garlic powder and salt together. Put the roast onto the wire rack in the roasting pan, fat side facing up and rib side facing down. Massage the roast with the prepared seasoning.

- Put in preheated oven and let it roast for 1 hour. Switch off the oven and don't take out the roast. Keep the oven door closed. Keep the roast inside the oven for 3 hours. Switch the oven back on at 375°F (190°C) temperature to reheat the roast 30-40 minutes before it's time to serve. The temperature inside the oven should not be less than 145°F (62°C). Take the roast out from the oven and let it sit for 10 minutes before slicing for serving.

Nutrition Information

- Calories: 576 calories;
- Total Fat: 46.2
- Sodium: 880
- Total Carbohydrate: 0.6
- Cholesterol: 137
- Protein: 37

Fresh Figs And Di Parma Pizza

Serving: 6

Ingredients

- 2 tablespoons all-purpose flour
- 1 (8 ounce) package fresh mozzarella cheese, sliced
- 4 thin slices prosciutto di Parma
- salt and freshly ground black pepper
- 4 leaves fresh basil
- 1/3 cup extra-virgin olive oil
- 1 clove garlic, minced
- 1 pinch red pepper flakes
- 2 fresh figs, each cut into 4 wedges
- 1 1/2 tablespoons balsamic vinegar
- 1 pound fresh pizza dough

Direction

- Preheat an oven to 260°C/500°F. Dust 2 tbsp. flour on pizza stone.

- In a bowl, mix red pepper flakes, garlic and 1/3 cup extra-virgin olive oil.
- Put figs in another bowl; sprinkle balsamic vinegar on top.
- Stretch dough on stone to 12-in. circle. Spread olive oil mixture on dough; add mozzarella cheese and figs.
- In preheated oven, bake for 12 minutes till crust browns lightly.
- Take pizza out of oven; top using prosciutto. Rest for 4 minutes then season with pepper and salt. Use basil to garnish; slice.

Nutrition Information

- Calories: 462 calories;
- Sodium: 677
- Total Carbohydrate: 42.7
- Cholesterol: 34
- Protein: 14.8
- Total Fat: 24.8

Fruit 'n' Honey Granola

Ingredients

- 1/3 cup canola oil

- 2/3 cup honey

- 4 cups quick cooking oats

- 1 cup chopped toasted almonds

- 1/4 cup toasted wheat germ

- 1/2 cup raisins

- 1/2 cup chopped dried pineapple

- 1/2 cup sweetened dried cranberries

- 1/2 cup chopped dried papaya

- 1/4 cup sunflower seeds

- 1/4 cup ground flax seeds

- 1 teaspoon cinnamon

- 1/2 teaspoon ground nutmeg

Direction

- Heat the oven to 150°C or 300°F; use parchment paper to line a big baking sheet.
- Combine honey, canola oil, nutmeg, cinnamon, flax seeds, sunflower seeds, wheat germ, almonds and oats in a big bowl. Spread this mix on the prepped baking sheet evenly while slightly pressing it down using the back of a spoon.
- In the preheated oven, bake for 20 minutes until brown slightly, then let it cool through.
- Crack cooled granola into big chunks in a big bowl. Combine together the papaya, sweetened dried cranberries, pineapple and raisins, then put the mix into an airtight container for storage.

Nutrition Information

- Calories: 247 calories;

- Sodium: 3

- Total Carbohydrate: 37.1

- Cholesterol: 0

- Protein: 5.4

- Total Fat: 10.3

Garlicky Vodka Alfredo

Ingredients

- 1 (16 ounce) package penne rigate
- kosher salt to taste
- ground white pepper to taste
- 10 leaves fresh basil, torn or shredded
- 1 tablespoon extra-virgin olive oil
- 7 cloves roasted garlic
- 1/2 cup butter
- 1 1/2 cups heavy cream
- 1/4 cup chicken stock
- 1/2 cup vodka
- 2 cups grated Parmesan cheese
- 1/2 cup grated Asiago cheese

Direction

- Bring lightly salted water in a large pot to a boil, cook pasta in boiling water for 8 to 10 minutes or until al dente; drain off water.

- Heat oil over medium heat in a large skillet; sauté garlic in heated oil for approximately 3 minutes. Mix in vodka, chicken stock, cream, and butter; bring mixture to a simmer. Add pepper, salt, Asiago cheese, and Parmesan cheese, mix. Stir pasta into the sauce until evenly coated. Let simmer for 3 minutes longer. Sprinkle pasta mixture with fresh basil before serving.

Nutrition Information

- Calories: 1284 calories;
- Sodium: 1276
- Total Carbohydrate: 88.1
- Cholesterol: 239
- Protein: 40
- Total Fat: 80.2

Genuine Egg Noodles

Serving: 5

Ingredients

- 1/4 teaspoon baking powder
- 3 eggs
- 2 cups Durum wheat flour
- 1/2 teaspoon salt
- water as needed

Direction

- Mix together baking powder, salt, and flour. Stir in a sufficient amount of water and eggs to form a workable dough. Knead the dough until stiff. Roll into a ball and slice into 4 portions. Work with 1/4 of the dough at a time, roll to flatten to about 1/8-inch, using flour as necessary, bottom and top, to avoid sticking. Peel up and roll from one end to the opposite end. Slice the roll into strips, 3/8-inch each. The length of the noodles should be about 4-

5-inch depending on the thinness it was initially flattened. Allow to dry for 1-3 hours.

- Cook like any pasta. Alternatively, you can cook the noodles fresh without drying it first, just ensure that the water is boiling and prevent it from sticking. This will take practice to do it right.

Nutrition Information

- Calories: 271 calories;
- Total Fat: 4.9
- Sodium: 294
- Total Carbohydrate: 46.6
- Cholesterol: 112
- Protein: 12.7

Ginger Glazed Mahi Mahi

Serving: 4

Ingredients

- 3 tablespoons honey
- 3 tablespoons soy sauce
- 3 tablespoons balsamic vinegar
- 1 teaspoon grated fresh ginger root
- 1 clove garlic, crushed or to taste
- 2 teaspoons olive oil
- 4 (6 ounce) mahi mahi fillets
- salt and pepper to taste
- 1 tablespoon vegetable oil

Direction

- Combine olive oil, garlic, ginger, balsamic vinegar, soy sauce and honey in a low glass dish.
- Add pepper and salt to the fish fillets to season them. Set them down into dish with the skin side facing downwards, in the case that there is skin.

- With the cover on, keep it marinating in the fridge for about 20 minutes.
- Pour in vegetable oil into a big skillet. At medium high heat, heat the oil up. Move the fish out of the dish, keeping the marinade.
- Insert the fish into skillet, frying for 4-6 minutes per side until you can use a fork to flake the fish with ease. During the process, turn it over one time.
- Transfer the fillets into a serving platter. Maintain the warmth. Empty the reserved marinade into skillet, heating it at medium heat until reduced into a consistent glaze.
- Put the glaze atop fish spoon by spoon before serving at once.

Nutrition Information

- Calories: 259 calories;
- Total Fat: 7
- Sodium: 830
- Total Carbohydrate: 16

- Cholesterol: 124

- Protein: 32.4

Gkai Kamin

Serving: 4

Ingredients

- 5 tablespoons peeled and chopped fresh turmeric
- 1 teaspoon whole white peppercorns
- 1 (2 to 3 pound) whole chicken
- 2 stalks lemon grass
- 12 cloves garlic
- 2 tablespoons salt

Direction

- Cut leafy tops and roots off lemon grass stalks. Pound pepper, turmeric, garlic, salt and lemongrass into a fine paste using a mortar and pestle.

- Slice open chicken lengthwise. Split into 2 pieces and wash thoroughly. With mixed spice paste, rub chicken. Chill to marinate for 4 hours to overnight.

- For 10 to 15 minutes, grill over moderate heat till equally brown and well done. Serve while hot.

Nutrition Information

- Calories: 407 calories;
- Total Fat: 21.7
- Sodium: 3608
- Total Carbohydrate: 11.2
- Cholesterol: 121
- Protein: 39.7

Glazed Corned Beef

Serving: 7

Ingredients

- 4 1/2 pounds corned beef, rinsed
- 1 cup water
- 1 cup apricot preserves
- 1/4 cup brown sugar
- 2 tablespoons soy sauce

Direction

- Preheat an oven to 175°C/350°F>
- Use nonstick cooking spray to coat big pan. Put corned beef in dish; add water. Tightly cover with aluminum foil; bake for 2 hours then drain liquid.
- Mix soy sauce, brown sugar and apricot preserves in small bowl; evenly spread apricot mixture on corned beef.

- Bake for 25-30 minutes at 175°C/350°F, uncovered, till meat is tender, occasionally basting with pan drippings.
- Across grain, slice corned beef; serve.

Nutrition Information

- Calories: 463 calories;
- Total Fat: 24.3
- Sodium: 1725
- Total Carbohydrate: 38.1
- Cholesterol: 125
- Protein: 23.8

Goat Cheese Stuffed Chicken

Serving: 4

Ingredients

Tomato Sauce:

- 2 tablespoons tomato paste
- 2 tablespoons chopped fresh thyme
- 1/2 teaspoon white sugar
- 1/4 teaspoon salt
- 1 (14 ounce) can diced tomatoes with basil, garlic, and oregano - drained
- 2 tablespoons extra-virgin olive oil
- 1/2 onion, chopped
- 3 cloves garlic, minced

Chicken:

- 1/2 teaspoon ground black pepper
- 2 tablespoons butter
- 1 teaspoon extra-virgin olive oil

- 4 skinless, boneless chicken breast halves
- 1 (4 ounce) log goat cheese, crumbled
- 2 green onions, diced
- 2 tablespoons chopped fresh thyme

Direction

- In a shallow dish, arrange tomatoes; use hand or potato masher to mash.

- In a saucepan, heat 2 tablespoons of oil over medium heat. Add the onion; stir and cook for 3-5 minutes until translucent and soft. Add garlic and cook for around a minute until it releases the fragrance. Put in salt, sugar, 2 tablespoons of thyme, tomato paste, and crushed tomatoes. Boil. Turn the heat down to low, simmer with a cover for 10 minutes until reaching sauce consistency. Take the sauce away from heat.

- Use plastic wrap to cover chicken breasts and put on a flat work surface. Use the smooth side of a meat mallet, pound firmly chicken to a 1/2-inch thickness.

- In a bowl, mix pepper, 2 tablespoons of thyme, green onions, and goat cheese. On the center of each chicken breast, place 1/4 of the mixture. Roll each chicken breast up and arrange onto a plate, seam-side-down.

- In a skillet, heat a teaspoon of oil and butter over medium heat. Add in chicken, seam-side-down; cook for about 5 minutes on each side until golden brown. Add the tomato sauce; turn the heat down to medium-low. Cover, then simmer for 5-7 minutes until the juices run clear and no pink remains in the center. An instant-read thermometer should display at least 74°C (165°F) when inserted into the center.

Nutrition Information

- Calories: 390 calories;

- Protein: 30.1

- Total Fat: 24.6

- Sodium: 826

- Total Carbohydrate: 12.4

- Cholesterol: 96

Gorgonzola And Wild Mushroom Risotto

Serving: 4

Ingredients

- 2 tablespoons crumbled Gorgonzola cheese, or to taste

- ground black pepper to taste

- 1 teaspoon truffle oil (optional)

- 1 chopped onion

- 2 shallots, minced

- 2 ounces dried chanterelle mushrooms

- 1 1/2 teaspoons butter

- 1 quart hot chicken stock

- 2 tablespoons heavy cream

- 1 clove garlic, minced

- 3 ounces sliced fresh button mushrooms

- 1 (12 ounce) package Arborio rice

- 1/2 cup dry white wine

Direction

- Soak chanterelle mushrooms in hot water, put on a cover, and reserve for half an hour to soften. When soft, take mushrooms off the water and cut; dispose the water.

- In a big saucepan, melt the butter together with truffle oil on moderately-high heat. Put in garlic, shallot and onion; cook and mix for 2 minutes till onion starts to soften. Put in fresh mushrooms and keep cooking till mushroom softens and starts to render liquid. Mix in chopped chanterelle mushrooms and let cook for an additional 3 minutes.

- Put in the Arborio rice; cook and mix for several minutes till rice is thoroughly covered with onion mixture and seems shiny. Mix in white wine and cook till almost evaporated.

- Lower the heat to moderate and put in a third of hot chicken stock. Cook and mix for 5 minutes till chicken stock has mostly soaked in. While mixing in chicken stock, risotto must be simmering gently. Put in 1/2 of the rest of the stock and mix for an additional 5 minutes. Lastly, put in the rest of the stock and keep cooking for an additional 5 minutes till risotto turns creamy and rice is soft. Rice must not be fully tender, but still has a bit of firmness once you bite into it. You may put in a bit of water if necessary to cook rice to this state.

- Take risotto off the heat and mix in Gorgonzola cheese and heavy cream. Season with pepper and salt to taste and serve.

Nutrition Information

- Calories: 545 calories;

- Cholesterol: 21

- Protein: 16.3

- Total Fat: 7.7

- Sodium: 755

- Total Carbohydrate: 91.3

Gourmet Pub Burgers

Serving: 6

Ingredients

- 1 egg

- 1 teaspoon minced garlic

- 1 pinch kosher salt

- 1 pinch ground black pepper

- 1 1/3 pounds ground beef

- 1/2 cup bread crumbs

- 1 shallot, minced

- 2 tablespoons Dijon mustard

- 6 slices pancetta

- 6 hamburger buns, split

Direction

- Mix black pepper, salt, garlic, egg, Dijon mustard, shallot, breadcrumbs and ground beef in a big bowl; refrigerate the mixture for 20 minutes – 2 hours to incorporate flavors.

- Shape ground mixture to 6 patties.

- Heat a skillet on medium heat; in 1 single layer, lay pancetta slices in the hot skillet. Cook for 3-5 minutes till pancetta starts to sweat. Take pancetta from the skillet; keep warm.

- Preheat a grill to medium heat; oil grate lightly.

- On the preheated grill, cook patties, 4 minutes per side to get medium-well burgers/or to desired degree of doneness. An instant-read thermometer inserted in middle should read 70°C/160°F.

- Put 1 burger on each of burns; put a pancetta slice over burger.

Nutrition Information

- Calories: 445 calories;

- Total Fat: 23

- Sodium: 781

- Total Carbohydrate: 31

- Cholesterol: 103

- Protein: 26.2

THANK YOU

Thank you for choosing *Gourmet Recipes for Beginners Dinner* for improving your cooking skills! I hope you enjoyed making the recipes as much as tasting them! If you're interested in learning new recipes and new meals to cook, go and check out the other books of the series.

CPSIA information can be obtained
at www.ICGtesting.com
Printed in the USA
BVHW091140030621
608729BV00005B/1711